Also by Jaroslaw Jankowski

Why Are We So Different?
Your Guide to the 16 Personality Types

Why are we so very different from one another? Why do we organise our lives in such disparate ways? Why are our modes of assimilating information so varied? Why are our approaches to decision-making so diverse? Why are our forms of relaxing and 'recharging our batteries' so dissimilar?

Your Guide to the 16 Personality Types will help you to understand both yourselves and other people better. It will aid you not only in avoiding any number of traps, but also in making the most of your personal potential, as well as in taking the right decisions about your education and career and in building healthy relationships with others. The book contains the ID16™© Personality Test, which will enable you to determine your own personality type. It also offers a comprehensive description of each of the sixteen types.

The Idealist

**Your Guide
to the INFP Personality Type**

The ID16™© Personality Types series

JAROSLAW JANKOWSKI
M.Ed., EMBA

This is a book which can help you exploit your potential more fully, build healthy relationships with other people and make the right decisions about your education and career. However, it should not be considered to be a substitute for expert physiological or psychiatric consultation. Neither the author nor the publisher accept any responsibility whatsoever for any detrimental effects which may result from the inappropriate use of this book.

ID16™© is an independent typology developed by Polish educator and manager Jaroslaw Jankowski and grounded in Carl Gustav Jung's theory. It should not be confused with the personality typologies and tests proposed by other authors or offered by other institutions.

Original title: Twój typ osobowości: Idealista (INFP)
Translated from the Polish by Caryl Swift
Proof reading: Lacrosse | experts in translation
Layout editing by Zbigniew Szalbot

Published by LOGOS MEDIA

© Jaroslaw Jankowski 2016-2023
All rights reserved

Paperback: ISBN 978-83-7981-069-7
EPUB: ISBN 978-83-7981-070-3
MOBI: ISBN 978-83-7981-071-0

Contents

Contents 5
Preface 7
ID16™© and Jungian Personality Typology 9
The Idealist (INFP) 14
    The Personality in a Nutshell 14
    General character traits 16
    Socially 22
    Work and career paths 26
    Potential strengths and weaknesses 29
    Personal development 32
    Well-known figures 35
The ID16™© Personality Types in a Nutshell 37
    The Administrator (ESTJ) 37
    The Advocate (ESFJ) 39

- The Animator (ESTP) 40
- The Artist (ISFP) 41
- The Counsellor (ENFJ) 43
- The Director (ENTJ) 44
- The Enthusiast (ENFP) 45
- The Idealist (INFP) 47
- The Innovator (ENTP) 48
- The Inspector (ISTJ) 50
- The Logician (INTP) 51
- The Mentor (INFJ) 52
- The Practitioner (ISTP) 54
- The Presenter (ESFP) 55
- The Protector (ISFJ) 57
- The Strategist (INTJ) 58

Additional information 60

- The four natural inclinations 60
- The approximate percentage of each personality type in the world population 62
- The approximate percentage of women and men of each personality type in the world population 63

Bibliography 65

Preface

The work in your hands is a compendium of knowledge on the *idealist*. It forms part of the *ID16**TM*© *Personality Types* series, which consists of sixteen books on the individual personality types and *Who Are You? The ID16**TM*© *Personality Test*, an introduction to the ID16TM© independent personality typology, which is based on the theory developed by Carl Gustav Jung.

As you explore this book on the *idealist*, you will find the answer to a number of crucial questions:
- How do *idealists* think and what do they feel? How do they make decisions? How do they solve problems? What makes them anxious? What do they fear? What irritates them?
- Which personality types are they happy to encounter on their road through life and

which ones do they avoid? What kind of friends, life partners and parents do they make? How do others perceive them?
- What are their vocational predispositions? What sort of work environment allows them to function most effectively? Which careers best suit their personality type?
- What are their strengths and what do they need to work on? How can they make the most of their potential and avoid pitfalls?
- Which famous people correspond to the *idealist*'s profile?

The book also contains the most essential information about the ID16™© typology.

We sincerely hope that it will help you in coming to know yourself and others better.

ID16™© and Jungian Personality Typology

ID16™© numbers among what are referred to as Jungian personality typologies, which draw on the theories developed by Carl Gustav Jung (1875-19161), a Swiss psychiatrist and psychologist and a pioneer of the 'depth psychology' approach.

On the basis of many years of research and observation, Jung came to the conclusion that the differences in people's attitudes and preferences are far from random. He developed a concept which is highly familiar to us today: the division of people into extroverts and introverts. In addition, he distinguished four personality functions, which form two opposing pairs: sensing-intuition and thinking-feeling. He also established that one function is dominant in each pair. He became convinced that each and every person's dominant functions are fixed and independent of external conditions and that, together, what they form is a personality type.

In 1938, two American psychiatrists, Horace Gray and Joseph Wheelwright, created the first personality test based on Jung's theories. It was designed to make it possible to determine the dominant functions within the three dimensions described by Jung, namely, **extraversion-introversion**, **sensing-intuition** and **thinking-feeling**. That first test became the inspiration for other researchers. In 1942, again in America, Isabel Briggs Myers and Katherine Briggs began using their own personality test, broadening Gray's and Wheelwright's classic, three-dimensional model to include a fourth: **judging-perceiving**. The majority of subsequent personality typologies and tests drawing on Jung's theories also take that fourth dimension into account. They include the American typology published by David W. Keirsey in 1978 and the personality test developed in the nineteen seventies by Aušra Augustinavičiūtė, a Lithuanian psychologist. Over the following decades, other European researchers followed in their footsteps, creating more four-dimensional personality typologies and tests for use in personal coaching and career counselling.

ID16$^{TM©}$ figures among that group. An independent typology developed by Polish educator and manager Jaroslaw Jankowski, it was published in the first decade of the twenty-first century. ID16$^{TM©}$ is based on Carl Jung's classic theory and, like other contemporary Jungian typologies, it follows a four-dimensional path, terming those dimensions the **four natural inclinations**. These inclinations are dichotomous in nature and the picture they provide gives us information regarding a person's personality type. Analysis of the first inclination is intended to determine the dominant **source of life energy**, this being either the exterior or the interior world. Analysis of the second inclination defines the dominant **mode of assimilating information**, which occurs via the senses or via intuition. Analysis of the third inclination supplies a description of the **decision-making mode**, where either mind or heart is dominant, while analysis of the fourth inclination produces a definition of the dominant **lifestyle** as either organised or spontaneous. The combination of all these natural inclinations results in **sixteen possible personality types**.

One remarkable feature of the ID16$^{TM©}$ typology is its practical dimension. It describes the individual personality types in action – at work, in daily life and in interpersonal relations. It neither concentrates on the internal dynamics of personality nor does it undertake any theoretical attempts at explaining or commenting on invisible, interior processes. The focus is turned more toward the ways in which a given personality type manifests itself externally and how it affects the surrounding world. This emphasis on the social aspect of personality places ID16$^{TM©}$ somewhat closer to the previously mentioned typology developed by Aušra Augustinavičiūtė.

Each of the ID16$^{TM©}$ personality types is the result of a given person's natural inclinations.

There is nothing evaluative or judgemental about ascribing a person to a given type, though. No particular personality type is 'better' or 'worse' than any other. Each type is quite simply different and each has its own potential strengths and weaknesses. ID16™© makes it possible to identify and describe those differences. It helps us to understand ourselves and discover our place in the world.

Familiarity with our personality profile enables us to make full use of our potential and work on the areas which might cause us trouble. It is an invaluable aid in everyday life, in solving problems, in building healthy relationships with other people and in making decisions relating to our education and careers.

Determining personality is a process which is neither arbitrary nor mechanical in nature. As the 'owner and user' of our personality, each and every one of us is fully capable of defining which type we belong to. The individual's role is thus pivotal. This self-identification can be achieved either by analysing the descriptions of the ID16™© personality types and steadily narrowing down the fields of choice or by taking the short cut provided by the ID16™© Personality Test.[1] The role played by each 'personality user' is equally crucial when it comes to the test, given that the outcome depends entirely on the answers they provide.

---

[1] The test can be found in *Why Are We So Different? Your Guide to the 16 Personality Types* by Jaroslaw Jankowski.

Identifying personality types helps us to know both ourselves and others. Nonetheless, it should not be treated as some kind of future-determining oracle. No personality type can ever justify our weaknesses or poor interpersonal relationships. It might, however, help us to understand their causes!

ID16™© treats personality type not as a static, genetic, pre-determined condition, but as a product of innate and acquired characteristics. As such, it is a concept which neither diminishes free will nor engages in pigeonholing people. What it does is open up new perspectives for us, encouraging us to work on ourselves and indicating the areas where that work is most needed.

The Idealist (INFP)

THE ID16™© PERSONALITY TYPOLOGY

The Personality in a Nutshell

Life motto: We CAN live differently.

In brief, *idealists* …

are sensitive, loyal, and creative. Living in accordance with the values they hold is of immense importance to them and they both manifest an interest in the reality of the spirit and delve deeply into the mysteries of life. Wrapped up in the world's problems and open to the needs of other people, they prize harmony and balance.

Idealists are romantic; not only are they able to show love, but they also need warmth and affection themselves. With their outstanding ability to read other people's feelings and emotions, they build healthy, profound and enduring relationships. They feel that they are on very shaky ground in situations of conflict and have no real resistance to stress and criticism.

The *idealist's* four natural inclinations:

- source of life energy: the interior world
- mode of assimilating information: intuition
- decision-making mode: the heart
- lifestyle: spontaneous

Similar personality types:

- the Mentor
- the Enthusiast
- the Counsellor

Statistical data:

- *idealists* constitute between one and four per cent of the global community
- women predominate among *idealists* (60 per cent)
- Thailand is an example of a nation corresponding to the *idealist's* profile[2]

---

[2] What this means is not that all the residents of Thailand fall within this personality type, but that Thai society as a whole possesses a great many of the character traits typical of the *idealist*.

The Four-Letter Code

In terms of Jungian personality typology, the universal four-letter code for the *idealist* is INFP.

General character traits

Idealists are people whose interior world is a rich one. They thirst to understand themselves and others, pondering over why people behave in one way rather than another. Although they sometimes give the impression of keeping their distance, they are actually very open to others, with a sincere interest in their problems and the ability to throw themselves wholeheartedly into solving them.

Idealists yearn for harmony; they seek peace and strive to ease conflicts. In leading their lives, they follow their ideals, which are of paramount significance to them – hence the name for this personality type. Their aims in life rarely coincide with those of the majority; material possessions, power, authority and influence completely fail to interest them.

Given the values they profess, *idealists* sometimes have a sense of isolation or alienation, yet they will almost never abandon their ideals, not even when adhering to them costs them dearly. There is simply no other choice for them: they have to be themselves. In their eyes, a life lived in opposition to their values is a life devoid of sense and meaning.

As others see them

Other people perceive *idealists* as unassuming, kind and always ready to offer a helping hand. They can give the impression of being shy, distant and indecisive and are often seen as people who will launch into a host of undertakings, but are incapable of seeing them through to the end. On the other hand, their natural sensitivity to the needs and feelings of others arouses widespread respect.

Idealists have a reputation for calmness. Yet they will never know interior peace, for they are genuinely wrapped up in the problems of the world and highly sensitive to manifestations of injustice. They believe that every human being has the right both to happiness and to be themselves and they yearn for peace, unity and a better world. As they see it, remaining true to their ideals is worth any and every sacrifice and acting at variance with their system of values engenders a deep-seated sense of guilt in them.

World view and priorities

Idealists never cease to delight in the beauty of the world and are unendingly amazed and astonished by the reality around them. They have the ability to see goodness and beauty everywhere and are fascinated by the world and its people alike. Their gaze is turned to the future and they have a driving urge towards self-improvement and self-development. With their love of tapping into the mysteries of life and exploring its meaning, they devote little attention to material concerns. Their most compelling need is to discover the meaning of life, and they are drawn to the world of the spirit. If they profess no particular faith, they tend to be beset by a feeling of emptiness, a sense that something is lacking.

With their inner desire to change reality and help other people, *idealists* often devote their free time to socially oriented activities such as working as a volunteer for charitable organisations. Indeed, they do so regardless of their jobs, even when they are professionally engaged in providing assistance to others. Helping their friends and acquaintances also claims their 'off-duty' hours.

Indefatigable in striving to achieve the aims they identify with, they are equally as persevering in their quest for truth. Before they enter any new information into their internal 'database', they run it through the filter of their system of values. This is their way of assessing whether or not it will prove helpful in seeking the meaning of life, changing the world or helping others. In assimilating new information, they associate and combine it with what they have previously learned and experienced, and they place a great deal of trust in their intuition.

Decisions

Idealists make decisions guided more by their hearts than their heads and, from their point of view, the most important issue is the way in which what they decide will affect their own lives and those of other people. Arguments of a purely logical nature carry no weight with them and they have very little confidence in deliberations conducted rationally and impersonally on the basis of hard facts alone. Before making a decision, they reflect and prepare at length.

They both perceive and value the individuality of every single person. As such, they will never impose their convictions on others and, by the same token, dislike it intensely when someone else makes any attempt to pressurise them or force something on them.

Creativity

In general, *idealists* are highly original and inventive people who derive enormous joy from the act of creating, which is, in fact, more important to them than either the end result of their efforts or other people's perception of it. As a rule, they are seen as remarkable and individual, despite not going out of their way in the slightest to be 'original'; indeed, they are often not even aware that they are perceived in that light.

Perception and thinking

Idealists are open to new ideas and extremely flexible. When they are part of a group, they will let others make the decisions, which might give some people the impression that they are indifferent. However, if it seems that a decision will run contrary to their convictions, they are quite capable of suddenly springing into action, protesting resolutely and even fighting to defend what they consider to be important – much to the astonishment of those around them.

Accommodating themselves to socially accepted norms and conventions can sometimes be a problem for *idealists,* and they also have a tendency to focus on information which concurs with their own world view and 'miss' or ignore data which go against it. When employing their highly particular defence mechanisms, they can become more and more enclosed within their own world and lose the ability to look at problems from a wider perspective. That situation, in turn, can have an adverse impact on their relationships with others, leading to a specific form of self-isolation.

Organisational modes

Idealists rarely pay too much attention to external appearances and the latest trends from the world of fashion do not hold the slightest fascination for them. They may also give the impression of being chaotic and unreliable. However, they take their lives and responsibilities extremely seriously, demand a great deal of themselves and hunger for self-improvement. Nonetheless, they tend to be so absorbed in breathing life into their visions that everyday routine activities may well slip from their minds entirely and their desks will then be left disorderly, their wastepaper bins will overflow and their cars will remain unwashed as a result. They also have no love of administration or paperwork and are far from happy to undertake tasks requiring them to operate on the basis of pure logic and hard facts. Managing their time and organising themselves are also problem areas for them.

Aware of these shortcomings, they make efforts to put various aspects of their lives in order and will normally renew those attempts repeatedly, though with varying results. When they find themselves in a strained or conflict situation, they are incapable of acting rationally and, at a loss as to how to behave, they may well do absolutely anything simply in order to extract themselves from their predicament.

Communication

As a rule, *idealists* are sparing in their use of words; they speak when they have something to say and dislike talking about themselves. On the other hand, they have the ability to describe complex concepts and phenomena simply and comprehensibly and will readily employ colourful comparisons and metaphors. They are well aware of the immense power of words and their potential impact on others.

Idealists love profound conversations with a small group of people. Idle chatter, gossip and exchanges of views about the weather are of no interest to them at all. They dislike crowds and make unwilling public speakers.

They handle the written word masterfully and are also superb listeners, skilled at reading between the lines. As a result, they will be able to say a great deal about someone after meeting them for the first time and are rarely mistaken, at that. Other people frequently find themselves better able to verbalise their own thoughts and feelings when they talk to *idealists*, who, with their ability to put their gift of empathy to good use, can be highly effective mentors. In helping others, they make no attempt to solve problems by logical and rational means such as analysing causes and establishing where blame lies. Instead, they study a given situation through the prism of feelings and endeavour to find a way to extinguish negative emotions, smooth out disputes and work towards a compromise.

In the face of stress

For *idealists*, the combination of their ongoing search for excellence and the uphill task they face in struggling to bring order to certain aspects of their lives, such as organising their time, is a constant source of frustration. On the whole, they cope badly with stress; it causes them to lose faith in their own powers and either leaves them incapable of making a decision or renders them likely to launch impulsively into ill-considered actions. Physical activity is often their favourite way of spending their leisure time.

Socially

Idealists understand others and are able to identify their feelings and motives. Loyal, faithful friends and wonderful listeners, they love helping other people and frequently put the needs of others before their own. They themselves are very unwilling to open up in front of people and, at times, even those closest to them will have trouble working out what is going on inside them.

Idealists believe that other people help us to know ourselves better. Healthy relationships with their nearest and dearest are vital to them; without them, they are incapable of being happy and enjoying life to the full. They set enormous store by symbols and gestures in their relationships and will sometimes also attach great importance to particular, individual modes of behaviour. As they see it, if someone behaves in a way which goes against the rules once, they are liable to behave like that again in the future.

They frequently display a tendency to idealise good people and demonise wrongdoers – their world can often be a clear-cut matter of black or white.

Amongst friends

Idealists are slow to strike up friendship, but the bonds they establish are deep and enduring. They demonstrate great warmth towards others, are extremely sensitive to their feelings and needs, and their attitude is one of acceptance. Ideal relationships matter to them enormously and they are capable of investing tremendous effort in them. They will go to any lengths to avoid conflicts and disagreeable conversations which might hurt someone.

The loyalties and bonds of their friendships remain strong, even when they are apart for a lengthy period. On the whole, they have only a few friends and are always ready to show them support and surround them with care. They value deep, genuine ties and their friendships will often endure for a lifetime. *Mentors*, *enthusiasts*, *artists* and other *idealists* figure most frequently as their friends;

seldom will *administrators*, *inspectors* or *animators* number amongst them.

As life partners

Idealists are made for marriage. Their relationships are extraordinarily enduring and they are far less likely than others to remain single by choice. By nature, they are both highly romantic and uncommonly faithful.

Family is one of the most important things in their lives, and they dream of ideal, harmonious and romantic relationships; indeed, they often struggle to reconcile their expectations with reality. They bestow remarkable respect, admiration and trust on their partner, showering them with compliments and showing them immense warmth. They, too, have a profound need for closeness and affection; however, they are neither possessive nor jealous and will never impose themselves or seek to restrict or subordinate their partner or attempt to create a dependency.

They will go to any lengths to ease conflicts within their relationship and avoid unpleasant or awkward subjects, preferring to remain silent about problems rather than air them. They take any critical word whatsoever very personally; even a minor comment or joke can cause them immense pain. To others, their reactions might seem excessive and inappropriate, but *idealists* really do have an extremely low threshold of tolerance for criticism, which is why they are easily hurt. This can constitute a serious problem in relationships with *strategists*, *inspectors*, *directors* and *administrators*, for whom criticism, conflict and open confrontation are a normal aspect of interpersonal relations.

The natural candidates for an *idealist's* life partner are people of a personality type akin to their own: *mentors*, *enthusiasts* or *counsellors*. Building mutual understanding and harmonious relations will be easier in a union of that kind. Nonetheless, experience has taught us that people are also capable of creating happy and successful relationships despite what would seem to be an evident typological incompatibility.

As parents

Idealists take to the role of parents like ducks to water and treat their responsibilities extremely seriously. They provide their children with friendship, a secure environment and a warm-hearted atmosphere, showing them tremendous affection and showering them with praise. Uncommonly devoted, loyal and loving, they protect and support their offspring no matter what the situation. In bringing them up, they tend to employ the positive reinforcements of encouragement and reward, rather than criticism and discipline, resorting to more radical means only when their own system of values is affronted by their children's behaviour. Even so, they are more than willing to leave disciplinary matters to their partner.

Idealists respect their children's individuality and are very unlikely to restrict them. They allow them to take part in making family decisions and respect what they say. Children brought up by *idealists* in a single-parent family, for instance, may sometimes lack clarity when it comes to the rules that make the world go round. However, they will never want for warmth, support, trust or the space to develop and, as adults, that is what they esteem their parents for most highly.

Work and career paths

Idealists are capable of carrying out a diverse range of tasks. However, not everything will provide them with the same satisfaction and they are at their happiest when they can do a job which reflects their personal convictions.

Success

To *idealists*, work is something more than simply a means of earning money. They perceive neither promotion nor high remuneration as synonymous with success, which, as they see it, lies in understanding the meaning of life and the possibility of fulfilling their calling. What they long to do is something they see as profoundly meaningful.

As part of a team

By nature, *idealists* are individualists and are happiest working independently. Nonetheless, if the need arises, they can also fit in with a team. They have no difficulty in adapting to new situations, cope well with change and like new ideas. However, they need some private space and dislike it when someone invades it or interrupts or disturbs them.

When they work as part of a group, they contribute a friendly atmosphere, supporting the other employees and helping the team to succeed in its undertakings. As a rule, they promote the principles of democratic decision making and believe that encouragement and persuasion can achieve more than criticism or pressure. They will do anything they can to avoid conflict within the team and refrain from criticising their colleagues. When forced to call someone's attention to something, they will often tread so carefully and diplomatically that the message they are trying to convey is barely communicated at all.

Companies and institutions

The optimum environment for *idealists* is one where they can proceed in line with their convictions and achieve the aims in which they believe. They fit in well in companies which accept their employees' individualism, but feel stifled in bureaucratic surroundings where the staff's activities are restricted by myriad rigid procedures. In general, they find routine and repetitive tasks hard to handle.

They are happiest working in social organisations or an academic environment and to all intents and purposes are completely unfit for the uniformed services.

Views on workplace hierarchy

Idealists give their esteem to superiors who have a moral backbone, like a creative approach to tasks, support the people they supervise and are not in the least obsessive about procedures, deadlines and formalities. Excessive control irritates them, as does the abuse of authority and power. They chafe at soulless bureaucracy and the treatment of people as cogs in a machine, and cannot abide it when profit and productivity take precedence over the good of the employees.

Preferences

When it comes to *idealists*, stereotyping, the simplification of reality and any attempt whatsoever at uniform treatment are like a red rag to a bull. They are in their element in situations demanding the solution of complex and intricate problems, but dislike working under time pressure; an unmoveable deadline will give them a strong sense of being hampered and restricted.

Professions

Knowledge of our own personality profile and natural preferences provides us with invaluable help in choosing the optimal path in our professional careers. Experience has shown that, while *idealists* are perfectly able to work and find fulfilment in a range of fields, their personality type naturally predisposes them to the following fields and professions:

- acting
- advisor
- artistic director
- blogger
- clergy
- consultant

- editor
- human resources
- interior designer
- journalist
- life coach
- mediator
- multimedia specialist
- musician
- physiotherapist
- psychiatrist
- psychologist
- project coordinator
- publisher
- scientist
- set decorator
- social activist
- social welfare
- teacher
- tertiary educator
- therapist
- translator
- visual artist
- vocational training
- writer

Potential strengths and weaknesses

Like any other personality type, *idealists* have their potential strengths and weaknesses and this potential can be cultivated in a variety of ways. *Idealists'* personal happiness and professional fulfilment depend on whether they make the most of the 'pluses' offered by their personality type and face up to its inherent dangers. Here, then, is a SUMMARY of those 'pluses' and dangers:

Potential strengths

Idealists possess extraordinary warmth and are happy to turn it to 'warming' others. By nature sensitive and caring, they have the ability to identify other people's needs. They are alert to any and every manifestation of injustice and seek to act on behalf of those who are wronged, used or abused. Their stable system of values, uncommon empathy and sincere interest in the fate of others predispose them to acting for the social good. Extremely faithful and loyal, they are able to build profound, stable and enduring relationships. At the same time, they neither impose themselves on other people nor restrict them. On the contrary, they bestow their trust on them and provide them with the space to develop. Being remarkably flexible, they cope extremely well with change.

Their characteristic tolerance and openness to others extends to those whom the majority of society has rejected, and they will find positive potential and good in everyone. With their uncanny gift of empathy, they are able to support other people, giving them heart and faith in their own powers. They are also superb listeners, perceiving the feelings and motives of others. Their skills include the ability to build compromise and mutual agreement, leaving everyone involved with a sense of satisfaction and the conviction that they have succeeded in achieving what they wanted. They have no difficulty in digesting complex theories and concepts and, at one and the same time, are highly creative and open to spiritual and artistic experiences. Indeed, they themselves are often artistically gifted. They are also capable of expressing their thoughts, particularly in writing.

Potential weaknesses

Idealists have a very low threshold of immunity to criticism, especially when it comes from those close to them. Even minor disapproving comments or gently caustic jokes can undermine their faith in themselves and cause them immense pain. Indeed, they will sometimes perceive critical allusions even when none are being made. Their tremendous loyalty and attachment to people means that they will frequently have problems with putting an end to harmful or toxic relationships. Expressing critical opinions and calling other people's attention to shortcomings also comes hard to them and they will sometimes even struggle to present their own point of view. When forced to address an issue critically, they will often tread so carefully that the person or people they are talking to will have difficulty in understanding what it is that they are actually trying to say. They cope extremely badly with situations of conflict and may respond by behaving irrationally or making sudden, ill-considered decisions.

The severity of their self-appraisal and their acute need for affirmation and positive reinforcement from others impedes their ability to function in neutral or cold environments, a situation which is only magnified in situations of open disapproval. They are incapable of keeping a cool head in stressful circumstances and can also be subject to excessive emotional swings. Although their ideas are highly creative, they can sometimes be unrealistic, since they often fail to take into account the limitations and imperfections present in the world, with the human fallibility factor being one such instance. They have a tendency to treat opinions which oppose their own as an attack on themselves and their values and, when it comes to new information, they are inclined only to take it on board if it concurs with their views; should it threaten their outlook, they might well suppress it entirely. This approach will sometimes lead them to isolate themselves and shut themselves off in their own world.

Personal development

Idealists' personal development depends on the extent to which they make use of their natural potential and surmount the dangers inherent in their personality type. What follows are some practical tips which, together, form a specific guide that we might call *The Idealist's Ten Commandments*.

Stop being afraid of conflict

When you find yourself in a situation of conflict, stop hiding your head in the sand and, instead, voice your point of view and feelings openly. Conflict very often helps us to identify problems and solve them.

Look at problems from a wider perspective

Try to look at issues through other people's eyes. Give various points of view consideration and keep different aspects of the matter in mind.

Don't condemn others to relying on guesswork

Tell people how you feel, what you are going through and what you desire. Stop dithering about whether or not to express your opinions, feelings and emotions and just go for it. You will be helping your colleagues and your nearest and dearest immensely when you do.

Be more practical

You have a natural inclination to come up with idealistic notions which sometimes have little in common with real life. Give some thought to the practical aspects and to how they can actually be accomplished in this imperfect world we live in.

Stop agonising over the plan and get going on the action

Instead of nit-picking over how you can improve on what you intend to do, simply get going and do it. Otherwise the day will come when you realise that you have spent your entire life perfecting your plans. Surely setting out to accomplish them and doing things well, but not necessarily to the point of sheer perfection, would be better than never doing anything at all?

Stop fearing ideas and opinions which are different from yours

Before you reject them, give them some consideration and try to understand them. Being open to the viewpoints of others is not synonymous with discarding your own.

Stop fearing criticism

Quell your fear of expressing your own critical opinions and of accepting criticism from others. Criticism can be constructive. There is no law which says that it has to mean attacking people or undermining their worth.

Stop blaming others for your problems

Who has the greatest influence over your life? Who is the person most competent to solve your problems? You, of course! Shift your focus away from external obstacles, setbacks and adversities, and concentrate on your strengths and making the most of their potential instead.

Make time for pleasure

Try to tear yourself away from your responsibilities from time to time and do something for the sheer pleasure, relaxation and fun of it. Physical activity and contact with the arts will help you to avoid reaching exhaustion point – and that can only make you more effective!

Be kinder to yourself

Ask yourself a couple of questions. Do you demand too much of yourself? Are you too severe in your self-appraisal? In both cases, the answer is most probably going to be 'yes'. Be more understanding of yourself and afford yourself the same solicitude that you give to the happiness and well-being of others.

Well-known figures

Below is a list of some well-known people who match the *idealist's* profile:
- **Laura Ingalls Wilder** (1867-1957); an American author whose books include the *Little House on the Prairie* series.
- **Albert Schweitzer** (1875-1965); a German Lutheran theologian, philosopher, music scholar, musician and physician, he founded a hospital in Gabon and was awarded the Nobel Peace Prize.
- **Alan Alexander Milne** (1882-1956); an English author whose works include the Winnie-the-Pooh books for children.
- **Carl Rogers** (1902-1987); an American psychologist, psychotherapist and one of the most important figures in the development of humanistic psychology.
- **George Orwell** (1903-1950); an English novelist, essayist, journalist and critic whose works include *Animal Farm*.
- **James Herriot** (James Alfred Wight; 1916-1995); a British veterinary surgeon and writer whose works include the *All Creatures Great and Small* series.

- **John F. Kennedy** (1917-1963); the 35th president of the United States.
- **Scott Bakula** (born in 1954); an American screen actor whose filmography includes the *Quantum Leap* TV series.
- **Lisa Kudrow** (born in 1963); an American screen actress whose filmography includes the *Friends* TV series.
- **Julia Roberts** (born in 1967); an American screen actress whose filmography includes *Pretty Woman* and *Erin Brokovitch*, for which she won an Oscar.
- **Gillian Anderson** (born in 1968); an American screen actress whose filmography includes *The X Files*.
- **Megan Follows** (born in 1968); a Canadian-American stage and screen actress whose filmography includes the title role in the *Anne of Green Gables* TV mini-series.
- **Fred Savage** (born in 1976); an American screen actor whose filmography includes *The Wonder Years*, he is also a director and producer.

The ID16™© Personality Types in a Nutshell

The Administrator (ESTJ)
Life motto: *We'll get the job done!*

Administrators are hard-working, responsible and extremely loyal. Energetic and decisive, they value order, stability, security and clear rules. They are matter-of-fact and businesslike, logical, rational and practical and possess the capability to assimilate large amounts of detailed information.

Superb organisers, they are intolerant of ineffectuality, wastefulness and slothfulness. True to their convictions and direct in their contact with others, they present their point of view decisively and openly express critical opinions, sometimes hurting other people as a result.

The *administrator*'s four natural inclinations:
- source of life energy: the exterior world
- mode of assimilating information: via the senses
- decision-making mode: the mind
- lifestyle: organised

Similar personality types:
- the Animator
- the Inspector
- the Practitioner

Statistical data:
- *administrators* constitute between ten and thirteen per cent of the global community
- men predominate among *administrators* (60 per cent)
- the United States is an example of a nation corresponding to the *administrator's* profile[3]

Find out more!
The Administrator. Your Guide to the ESTJ Personality Type by Jaroslaw Jankowski

---

[3] What this means is not that all the residents of the USA fall within this personality type, but that American society as a whole possesses a great many of the character traits typical of the *administrator*.

The Advocate (ESFJ)

Life motto: *How can I help you?*

Advocates are well-organised, energetic and enthusiastic. Practical, responsible and conscientious, they are sincere and exceptionally gregarious.

Advocates are perceptive of human feelings, emotions and needs. They value harmony and find criticism and conflict difficult to bear. With their sensitivity to any and every manifestation of injustice, prejudice or detriment to another, they are genuinely interested in other people's problems and take real delight in helping them and tending to their needs, while often neglecting their own. They have a tendency to do everything for others and can be vulnerable to manipulation.

The *advocate*'s four natural inclinations:

- source of life energy: the exterior world
- mode of assimilating information: via the senses
- decision-making mode: the heart
- lifestyle: organised

Similar personality types:

- the Presenter
- the Protector
- the Artist

Statistical data:

- *advocates* constitute between ten and thirteen per cent of the global community
- women predominate among *advocates* (70 per cent)
- Canada is an example of a nation corresponding to the *advocate's* profile

Find out more!

The Advocate. Your Guide to the ESFJ Personality Type by Jaroslaw Jankowski

The Animator (ESTP)

Life motto: *Let's DO something!*

Animators are energetic, active and enterprising. Fond of the company of others, they have the ability to enjoy the moment and are spontaneous, flexible and open to change.

Animators are inspirers and instigators, spurring others to act. Being logical, rational and pragmatic realists, they are wearied by abstract concepts and solutions for the future. Their focus is on solving concrete problems in the here and now. They have difficulties with organising and planning and can be impulsive, acting first and thinking later.

The *animator's* four natural inclinations:

- source of life energy: the exterior world
- mode of assimilating information: via the senses

- decision-making mode: the mind
- lifestyle: spontaneous

Similar personality types:
- the Administrator
- the Practitioner
- the Inspector

Statistical data:
- *animators* constitute between six and ten per cent of the global community
- men predominate among *animators* (60 per cent)
- Australia is an example of a nation corresponding to the *animator's* profile

Find out more!
The Animator. Your Guide to the ESTP Personality Type by Jaroslaw Jankowski

The Artist (ISFP)
Life motto: *Let's create something!*

Artists are sensitive, creative and original, with a sense of the aesthetic and natural artistic talents. Independent in character, they follow their own system of values and are optimistic in outlook, with a positive approach to life and an ability to enjoy the moment.

Helping others is a source of joy to them. They find abstract theories tedious and would rather create reality than talk about it, although starting on something new comes more easily to them than finishing what they have already started. They have difficulty in voicing their own desires and needs.

The *artist's* four natural inclinations:
- source of life energy: the interior world
- mode of assimilating information: via the senses
- decision-making mode: the heart
- lifestyle: spontaneous

Similar personality types:
- the Protector
- the Presenter
- the Advocate

Statistical data:
- *artists* constitute between six and nine per cent of the global community
- women predominate among *artists* (60 per cent)
- China is an example of a nation corresponding to the *artist's* profile

Find out more!
The Artist. Your Guide to the ISFP Personality Type by Jaroslaw Jankowski

The Counsellor (ENFJ)

Life motto: *My friends are my world*

Counsellors are optimistic, enthusiastic and quick-witted. Courteous and tactful, they have an extraordinary gift for empathy and find joy in acting for the good of others, with no thought of themselves. They have the ability to influence other people, inspiring them, eliciting their hidden potential and giving them faith in their own powers. Radiating warmth, they draw others to them and often help them in solving their personal problems.

Counsellors can be over-trusting and have a tendency to view the world through rose-tinted glasses. With their focus on other people, they often forget about their own needs.

The *counsellor's* four natural inclinations:

- source of life energy: the exterior world
- mode of assimilating information: intuition
- decision-making mode: the heart
- lifestyle: organised

Similar personality types:

- the Enthusiast
- the Mentor
- the Idealist

Statistical data:
- *counsellors* constitute between three and five per cent of the global community
- women predominate among *counsellors* (80 per cent)
- France is an example of a nation corresponding to the *counsellor's* profile

Find out more!
The Counsellor. Your Guide to the ENFJ Personality Type by Jaroslaw Jankowski

The Director (ENTJ)
Life motto: *I'll tell you what you need to do.*

Directors are independent, active and decisive. Rational, logical and creative, when they analyse problems they look at the wider picture and are able to foresee the future consequences of human activities. They are characterised by optimism and a healthy sense of their own worth and are capable of transforming theoretical concepts into concrete, practical plans of action.

Visionaries, mentors and organisers, *directors* possess natural leadership skills. Their powerful personalities and direct and critical style can often have an intimidating effect, causing them problems in their interpersonal relationships.

The *director's* four natural inclinations:
- source of life energy: the exterior world

- mode of assimilating information: intuition
- decision-making mode: the mind
- lifestyle: organised

Similar personality types:
- the Innovator
- the Strategist
- the Logician

Statistical data:
- *directors* constitute between two and five per cent of the global community
- men predominate among *directors* (70 per cent)
- Holland is an example of a nation corresponding to the *director's* profile

Find out more!
The Director. Your Guide to the ENTJ Personality Type by Jaroslaw Jankowski

The Enthusiast (ENFP)

Life motto: *We'll manage!*

Enthusiasts are energetic, enthusiastic and optimistic. Capable of enjoying life and looking ahead to the future, they are dynamic, quick-witted and creative. They have a liking for people in general, value honest and genuine relationships and are warm, sincere and emotional. Criticism is something they handle badly. With their gift for empathy and ability to perceive people's needs, feelings and motives, they both inspire others and infect them with their own enthusiasm.

They love to be at the centre of events and are flexible and capable of improvising. Their inclination leads towards idealistic notions. Being easily distracted, they have problems with seeing things through to the end.

The *enthusiast's* four natural inclinations:

- source of life energy: the exterior world
- mode of assimilating information: intuition
- decision-making mode: the heart
- lifestyle: spontaneous

Similar personality types:

- the Counsellor
- the Idealist
- the Mentor

Statistical data:

- *enthusiasts* constitute between five and eight per cent of the global community
- women predominate among *enthusiasts* (60 per cent)
- Italy is an example of a nation corresponding to the *enthusiast's* profile

Find out more!

The Enthusiast. Your Guide to the ENFP Personality Type by Jaroslaw Jankowski

The Idealist (INFP)

Life motto: *We CAN live differently.*

Idealists are sensitive, loyal, and creative. Living in accordance with the values they hold is of immense importance to them and they both manifest an interest in the reality of the spirit and delve deeply into the mysteries of life. Wrapped up in the world's problems and open to the needs of other people, they prize harmony and balance.

Idealists are romantic; not only are they able to show love, but they also need warmth and affection themselves. With their outstanding ability to read other people's feelings and emotions, they build healthy, profound and enduring relationships. They feel that they are on very shaky ground in situations of conflict and have no real resistance to stress and criticism.

The *idealist's* four natural inclinations:

- source of life energy: the interior world
- mode of assimilating information: intuition
- decision-making mode: the heart
- lifestyle: spontaneous

Similar personality types:
- the Mentor
- the Enthusiast
- the Counsellor

Statistical data:
- *idealists* constitute between one and four per cent of the global community
- women predominate among *idealists* (60 per cent)
- Thailand is an example of a nation corresponding to the *idealist's* profile

Find out more!
The Idealist. Your Guide to the INFP Personality Type by Jaroslaw Jankowski

The Innovator (ENTP)

Life motto: *How about trying a different approach...?*

Innovators are inventive, original and independent. Optimistic, energetic and enterprising, they are people of action who love being at the centre of events and solving 'insoluble' problems. Their thoughts are turned to the future and they are curious about the world and visionary by nature. Open to new concepts and ideas, they enjoy new experiences and experiments and have the ability to identify the connections between separate events.

Innovators are spontaneous, communicative and self-assured. However, they tend to overestimate their own possibilities and have problems with seeing things through to the end. They are also inclined to be impatient and to take risks.

The *innovator's* four natural inclinations:

- source of life energy: the exterior world
- mode of assimilating information: intuition
- decision-making mode: the mind
- lifestyle: spontaneous

Similar personality types:

- the Director
- the Logician
- the Strategist

Statistical data:

- *innovators* constitute between three and five per cent of the global community
- men predominate among *innovators* (70 per cent)
- Israel is an example of a nation corresponding to the *innovator's* profile

Find out more!

The Innovator. Your Guide to the ENTP Personality Type by Jaroslaw Jankowski

The Inspector (ISTJ)

Life motto: *Duty first.*

Inspectors are people who can always be counted on. Well-mannered, punctual, reliable, conscientious and responsible, when they give their word, they keep it. Being analytical, methodical, systematic and logical by nature, they tend be seen as serious, cold and reserved. They prize calm, stability and order, have no fondness for change and like clear principles and concrete rules.

Inspectors are hard-working, persevering and capable of seeing things through to the end. As perfectionists, they try to exercise control over everything within their sphere and are sparing in their praise. They also underrate the importance of other people's feelings and emotions.

The *inspector's* four natural inclinations:

- source of life energy: the interior world
- mode of assimilating information: via the senses
- decision-making mode: the mind
- lifestyle: organised

Similar personality types:

- the Practitioner
- the Administrator
- the Animator

Statistical data:

- *inspectors* constitute between six and ten per cent of the global community
- men predominate among *inspectors* (60 per cent)
- Switzerland is an example of a nation corresponding to the *inspector's* profile

Find out more!

The Inspector. Your Guide to the ISTJ Personality Type by Jaroslaw Jankowski

The Logician (INTP)

Life motto: *Above all else, seek to discover the truths about the world.*

Logicians are original, resourceful and creative. With a love for solving problems of a theoretical nature, they are analytical, quick-witted, enthusiastically disposed towards new concepts and have the ability to connect individual phenomena, educing general rules and theories from them. Logical, exact and inquiring, they are quick to spot incoherence and inconsistency.

Logicians are independent, sceptical of existing solutions and authorities, tolerant and open to new challenges. When immersed in thought, they will sometimes lose touch with the outside world.

The *logician's* four natural inclinations:

- source of life energy: the interior world
- mode of assimilating information: intuition
- decision-making mode: the mind
- lifestyle: spontaneous

Similar personality types:

- the Strategist
- the Innovator
- the Director

Statistical data:

- *logicians* constitute between two and three per cent of the global community;
- men predominate among *logicians* (80 per cent)
- India is an example of a nation corresponding to the *logician's* profile

Find out more!

The Logician. Your Guide to the INTP Personality Type by Jaroslaw Jankowski

The Mentor (INFJ)

Life motto: *The world CAN be a better place!*

Mentors are creative and sensitive. With their gaze fixed firmly on the future, they spot opportunities and potential imperceptible to others. Idealists and visionaries, they are geared towards helping people and are conscientious, responsible and, at one and the same time, courteous, caring and friendly. They strive to understand the mechanisms governing the world and view problems from a wide perspective.

Superb listeners and observers, *mentors* are characterised by their extraordinary empathy, intuition and trust of people and are capable of reading the feelings and emotions of others. They find criticism and conflict difficult to bear and can come across as enigmatic.

The *mentor's* four natural inclinations:

- source of life energy: the interior world
- mode of assimilating information: intuition
- decision-making mode: the heart
- lifestyle: organised

Similar personality types:

- the Idealist
- the Counsellor
- the Enthusiast

Statistical data:

- *mentors* constitute one per cent of the global community and are the most rarely occurring of the sixteen personality types
- women predominate among *mentors* (80 per cent)

- Norway is an example of a nation corresponding to the *mentor's* profile

Find out more!
The Mentor. Your Guide to the INFJ Personality Type by Jaroslaw Jankowski

The Practitioner (ISTP)
Life motto: *Actions speak louder than words.*

Practitioners are optimistic and spontaneous, with a positive approach to life. Reserved and independent, they hold true to their personal convictions and view external principles and norms with scepticism. They find abstract concepts and solutions for the future tiresome and would far rather roll up their sleeves and get to work on solving tangible and concrete problems.

Adapting well to new places and situations, they enjoy fresh challenges and risks and are capable of keeping a cool head in the face of threats and danger. Their general reticence and extreme reserve when it comes to expressing their opinions mean that other people may often find them impenetrable.

The *practitioner's* four natural inclinations:
- source of life energy: the interior world
- mode of assimilating information: via the senses

- decision-making mode: the mind
- lifestyle: spontaneous

Similar personality types:
- the Inspector
- the Animator
- the Administrator

Statistical data:
- *practitioners* constitute between six and nine per cent of the global community
- men predominate among *practitioners* (60 per cent)
- Singapore is an example of a nation corresponding to the *practitioner's* profile

Find out more!

The Practitioner. Your Guide to the ISTP Personality Type by Jaroslaw Jankowski

The Presenter (ESFP)

Life motto: *Now is the perfect moment!*

Presenters are optimistic, energetic and outgoing, with the ability to enjoy life and have fun to the full. Practical, flexible and spontaneous at one and the same time, they enjoy change and new experiences, coping badly with solitude, stagnation and routine.

With their liking for being at the centre of attention, they are natural-born actors and their speaking abilities arouse the interest and enthusiasm of their listeners. Focused as they are on the present moment, they will sometimes lose sight of their long-term aims and can also have problems with foreseeing the consequences of their actions.

The *presenter's* four natural inclinations:

- source of life energy: the exterior world
- mode of assimilating information: via the senses
- decision-making mode: the heart
- lifestyle: spontaneous

Similar personality types:

- the Advocate
- the Artist
- the Protector

Statistical data:

- *presenters* constitute between eight and thirteen per cent of the global community
- women predominate among *presenters* (60 per cent)
- Brazil is an example of a nation corresponding to the *presenter's* profile

Find out more!

The Presenter. Your Guide to the ESFP Personality Type by Jaroslaw Jankowski

The Protector (ISFJ)

Life motto: *Your happiness matters to me.*

Protectors are sincere, warm-hearted, unassuming, trustworthy and extraordinarily loyal. With their ability to perceive people's needs and their desire to help them, they will always put others first. Practical, well-organised and gifted with both an eye and a memory for detail, they are responsible, hard-working, patient, persevering and capable of seeing things through to the end.

Protectors set great store by tranquillity, stability and friendly relations with others and are skilled at building bridges between people. By the same token, they find conflict and criticism difficult to bear. Given their powerful sense of duty and their constant readiness to come to the aid of others, they can end up being used by people.

The *protector's* four natural inclinations:

- source of life energy: the interior world
- mode of assimilating information: via the senses
- decision-making mode: the heart
- lifestyle: organised

Similar personality types:

- the Artist
- the Advocate
- the Presenter

Statistical data:
- *protectors* constitute between eight and twelve per cent of the global population
- women predominate among *protectors* (70 per cent)
- Sweden is an example of a nation corresponding to the *protector's* profile

Find out more!
The Protector. Your Guide to the ISFJ Personality Type by Jaroslaw Jankowski

The Strategist (INTJ)

Life motto: *I can certainly improve this.*

Strategists are independent and outstandingly individualistic, with an immense seam of inner energy. Creative, inventive and resourceful, others perceive them as competent, self-assured and, at one and the same time, distant and enigmatic. No matter what they turn their attention to, they will always look at the bigger picture and they have a driving urge to improve the world around them and set it in order.

Well-organised, responsible, critical and demanding, they are difficult to knock off balance – and just as hard to please to the full. Reading the emotions and feelings of others is something they find very problematic.

The *strategist's* four natural inclinations:

- source of life energy: the interior world
- mode of assimilating information: intuition
- decision-making mode: the mind
- lifestyle: organised

Similar personality types:

- the Logician
- the Director
- the Innovator

Statistical data:

- *strategists* constitute between one and two per cent of the global community
- men predominate among *strategists* (80 per cent)
- Finland is an example of a nation corresponding to the *strategist's* profile

Find out more!

The Strategist. Your Guide to the INTJ Personality Type by Jaroslaw Jankowski

Additional information

The four natural inclinations

1. THE DOMINANT SOURCE OF LIFE ENERGY

    a. THE EXTERIOR WORLD
    People who draw their energy from outside. They need activity and contact with others and find being alone for any length of time hard to bear.

    b. THE INTERIOR WORLD
    People who draw their energy from their inner world. They need quiet and solitude and feel drained

when they spend any length of time in a group.

2. THE DOMINANT MODE OF ASSIMILATING INFORMATION

   a. VIA THE SENSES
   People who rely on the five senses and are persuaded by facts and evidence. They have a liking for methods and practices which are tried and tested and prefer concrete tasks and are realists who trust in experience.

   b. VIA INTUITION
   People who rely on the sixth sense and are driven by what they 'feel in their bones'. They have a liking for innovative solutions and problems of a theoretical nature and are characterised by a creative approach to their tasks and the ability to predict.

3. THE DOMINANT DECISION-MAKING MODE

   a. THE MIND
   People who are guided by logic and objective principles. They are critical and direct in expressing their opinions.

b. THE HEART
People who are guided by their feelings and values. They long for harmony and mutual understanding with others.

4. THE DOMINANT LIFESTYLE

   a. ORGANISED
   People who are conscientious and organised. They value order and like to operate according to plan.

   b. SPONTANEOUS
   People who are spontaneous and value freedom of action. They live for the moment and have no trouble finding their feet in new situations.

The approximate percentage of each personality type in the world population

Personality Type:	Proportion:
• The Administrator (ESTJ):	10-13%
• The Advocate (ESFJ):	10-13%
• The Animator (ESTP):	6-10%
• The Artist (ISFP):	6-9%
• The Counsellor (ENFJ):	3-5 %
• The Director (ENTJ):	2-5%

- The Enthusiast (ENFP): 5-8%
- The Idealist (INFP): 1-4%
- The Innovator (ENTP): 3-5%
- The Inspector (ISTJ): 6-10%
- The Logician (INTP): 2-3%
- The Mentor (INFJ): ca. 1%
- The Practitioner (ISTP): 6-9%
- The Presenter (ESFP): 8-13%
- The Protector (ISFJ): 8-12%
- The Strategist (INTJ): 1-2%

The approximate percentage of women and men of each personality type in the world population

Personality Type: **Women / Men:**

- The Administrator (ESTJ): 40% / 60%
- The Advocate (ESFJ): 70% / 30%
- The Animator (ESTP): 40% / 60%
- The Artist (ISFP): 60% / 40%
- The Counsellor (ENFJ): 80% / 20%
- The Director (ENTJ): 30% / 70%
- The Enthusiast (ENFP): 60% / 40%
- The Idealist (INFP): 60% / 40%
- The Innovator (ENTP): 30% / 70%
- The Inspector (ISTJ): 40% / 60%
- The Logician (INTP): 20% / 80%
- The Mentor (INFJ): 80% / 20%
- The Practitioner (ISTP): 40% / 60%
- The Presenter (ESFP): 60% / 40%

THE IDEALIST

- The Protector (ISFJ):   70% / 30%
- The Strategist (INTJ): 20% / 80%

Bibliography

- Arraj, Tyra & Arraj, James: *Tracking the Elusive Human, Volume 1: A Practical Guide to C.G. Jung's Psychological Types, W.H. Sheldon's Body and Temperament Types and Their Integration*, Inner Growth Books, 1988
- Arraj, James: *Tracking the Elusive Human, Volume 2: An Advanced Guide to the Typological Worlds of C. G. Jung, W.H. Sheldon, Their Integration, and the Biochemical Typology of the Future*, Inner Growth Books, 1990
- Berens, Linda V.; Cooper, Sue A.; Ernst, Linda K.; Martin, Charles R.; Myers, Steve; Nardi, Dario; Pearman, Roger R.; Segal, Marci; Smith, Melissa: *A Quick Guide to the 16 Personality Types in Organizations: Understanding Personality Differences in the Workplace*, Telos Publications, 2002

- Geier, John G. & Downey, E. Dorothy: *Energetics of Personality*, Aristos Publishing House, 1989
- Hunsaker, Phillip L. & Alessandra, Anthony J.: *The Art of Managing People*, Simon and Schuster, 1986
- Jung, Carl Gustav: *Psychological Types (The Collected Works of C. G. Jung, Vol. 6)*, Princeton University Press, 1976
- Kise, Jane A. G.; Stark, David & Krebs Hirsch, Sandra: *LifeKeys: Discover Who You Are*, Bethany House, 2005
- Kroeger, Otto & Thuesen, Janet: *Type Talk or How to Determine Your Personality Type and Change Your Life*, Delacorte Press, 1988
- Lawrence, Gordon: *People Types and Tiger Stripes*, Center for Applications of Psychological Type, 1993
- Lawrence, Gordon: *Looking at Type and Learning Styles*, Center for Applications of Psychological Type, 1997
- Maddi, Salvatore R.: *Personality Theories: A Comparative Analysis*, Waveland, 2001
- Martin, Charles R.: *Looking at Type: The Fundamentals Using Psychological Type To Understand and Appreciate Ourselves and Others*, Center for Applications of Psychological Type, 2001
- Meier C.A.: Personality: *The Individuation Process in the Light of C. G. Jung's Typology*, Daimon Verlag, 2007

- Pearman, Roger R. & Albritton, Sarah: *I'm Not Crazy, I'm Just Not You: The Real Meaning of the Sixteen Personality Types*, Davies-Black Publishing, 1997
- Segal, Marci: Creativity and Personality Type: *Tools for Understanding and Inspiring the Many Voices of Creativity*, Telos Publications, 2001
- Sharp, Daryl: Personality Type: *Jung's Model of Typology*, Inner City Books, 1987
- Spoto, Angelo: *Jung's Typology in Perspective*, Chiron Publications, 1995
- Tannen, Deborah: *You Just Don't Understand*, William Morrow and Company, 1990
- Thomas, Jay C. & Segal, Daniel L.: *Comprehensive Handbook of Personality and Psychopathology, Personality and Everyday Functioning*, Wiley, 2005
- Thomson, Lenore: *Personality Type: An Owner's Manual*, Shambhala, 1998
- Tieger, Paul D. & Barron-Tieger Barbara: *Just Your Type: Create the Relationship You've Always Wanted Using the Secrets of Personality Type*, Little, Brown and Company, 2000
- Von Franz, Marie-Louise & Hillman, James: *Lectures on Jung's Typology*, Continuum International Publishing Group, 1971

Putting the Reader first.

An Author Campaign Facilitated by ALLi.

www.ingramcontent.com/pod-product-compliance
Lightning Source LLC
Chambersburg PA
CBHW031208020426
42333CB00013B/850